BUSH SCENES and BIRDS of PERTH and SURROUNDS
by Brian Sanger

National Library of Australia Cataloguing-in-Publication entry

Author: Sanger, Brian, 1939- author, photographer.
Title: Bush scenes and birds of Perth and surrounds / by Brian Sanger ;
              David Solly Sandler, compiler.
ISBN: 9780992468439 (paperback)
Series: Photographic art of Brian Sanger.
Subjects: Sanger, Brian, 1939-
              Photography, Artistic.
              Outdoor photography--Western Australia--Perth Region.
              Nature photography--Western Australia--Perth Region.
              Photography of birds--Western Australia--Perth Region.
              Fantasy in art.
              Perth Region (W.A.)--Pictorial works.
Other Authors/Contributors:
              Sandler, David Solly, compiler.
Dewey Number: 778.71

Brian Sanger.

BRIAN SANGER   Photographic Artist

I was born in London in 1939 and remember when I was very young trying to paint a white cat black so it would not stand out during the black outs near the end of the war.

As far as I remember I always liked art. I took art at school but I never had any formal qualifications.

While in my twenties I started taking an interest in photography.

I came to Australia in 1973 with my wife and two young sons and fell in love with the landscape.

Art and photography has been my hobby for many years and even more so since I retired and in the past few years I have taken to combining my photos and art on the computer and my speciality is creating fantasy art and nature working on the computer.